VOICES of FREEDOM

English and Civics for U.S. Citizenship

FOURTH EDITION

Bill Bliss

PEARSON
Longman

Dedicated to Benjamin and Flora Bliss, Nathan and Sophia Bliss, and Nat and Betty Meister.

Voices of Freedom: English and Civics for U.S. Citizenship, Activity & Test Prep Workbook

Copyright © 2012 by Pearson Education, Inc.
Pearson Education, Inc.
All rights reserved.

No part of this publication may be reproduced, stored in a retrieval system, or transmitted in any form or by any means, electronic, mechanical, photocopying, recording, or other without the prior permission of the publisher.

Pearson Education, 10 Bank Street, White Plains, NY 10606

Editorial director: Pam Fishman
Director of special projects and digital initiatives: Aliza Greenblatt
Manager of electronic production services: Warren Fischbach
Associate managing editor: Robert Ruvo
Director of prepress: Liza Pleva
Senior procurement specialist: Dave Dickey
Text and cover design: Wendy Wolf
Text composition: TSI Graphics
Cover image: Shutterstock and Getty Images, Inc./Purestock.
Illustrations: Richard E. Hill

ISBN-10: 0-13-286206-9
ISBN-13: 978-0-13-286206-6

PEARSON LONGMAN ON THE **WEB**

Pearsonlongman.com offers online resources for teachers and students. Access our Companion Websites, our online catalog, and our local offices around the world.

Visit us at **pearsonlongman.com**.

Printed in the United States of America
1 2 3 4 5 6 7 8 9 10 — V001 — 16 15 14 13 12 11

CONTENTS

*See the Correlation Key on the next page for a listing of student book units, the English Speaking Test Prep student book pages recommended for each unit, and the corresponding Interview Practice lessons in this workbook.

INTERVIEW PRACTICE CORRELATION KEY

UNIT	OBJECTIVES	STUDENT TEXT	WORKBOOK
Unit A	Identifying what to bring to the USCIS interview; Arriving at the USCIS office; Checking in; Greeting the USCIS officer; Walking to the office; Swearing in; Presenting your identification	pp. 213–215	Interview Practice 1–6
Unit B	Identifying requirements of the English Speaking Test; Asking for repetition; Showing confidence and pride during the interview; Giving information about name, other names used, or the desire to change name; Giving information about eligibility for citizenship	pp. 216–217	Interview Practice 7–10
Unit 1	Giving information about yourself; Giving information about address and telephone numbers; Asking for clarification; Saying you don't understand	pp. 218–219 (Sections 7–8)	Interview Practice 11–16
Unit 2	Giving information for criminal records search: height, weight, race, hair color, eye color	p. 219 (Section 9)	Interview Practice 17–18
Unit 3	Asking the officer to paraphrase a question; Giving information about residence and employment; Talking about time outside the United States	pp. 220–221	Interview Practice 19–21
Unit 4	Recognizing how the USCIS officer might check the applicant's understanding; Asking for an explanation or paraphrasing; Giving information about marital history and children	p. 222	Interview Practice 22
Unit 5	Answering Form N-400 "Part 10" Questions 1–6	p. 223	Interview Practice 23–25
Unit 6	Answering Form N-400 "Part 10" Questions 7–10	pp. 223–224	Interview Practice 26–28
Unit 7	Answering Form N-400 "Part 10" Questions 11–16	p. 224	Interview Practice 29–31
Unit 8	Answering Form N-400 "Part 10" Questions 17–20	p. 224	Interview Practice 32–34
Unit 9	Answering Form N-400 "Part 10" Questions 21–22e	p. 224	Interview Practice 35–37
Unit 10	Answering Form N-400 "Part 10" Questions 22f–25	pp. 224–225	Interview Practice 38–40
Unit 11	Answering Form N-400 "Part 10" Questions 29–33	p. 225	Interview Practice 41–43
Unit 12	Answering Form N-400 "Part 10" Questions 34–39	p. 225	Interview Practice 44–46

To the Teacher

The new edition of *Voices of Freedom* prepares students for the civics and English requirements of the new U.S. citizenship test. The text also serves as a basic course for students in EL/Civics programs. It is designed for students at low-beginning, beginning, and low-intermediate levels whose limited language skills prevent them from using standard civics materials.

The lessons in the new *Voices of Freedom* Activity & Test Prep Workbook are fully coordinated with the units in the student book and with the English Test practice sections in the appendix. They are designed to help students develop the civics knowledge and the reading, writing, and interview skills they need for success in their citizenship exam and USCIS interview for naturalization.

WRITING PRACTICE

Writing Practice lessons offer students fundamental practice tracing and copying letters, numbers, words, and sentences. The lessons for preparatory Units A and B provide students with practice writing the alphabet, numbers, months, and dates. The lessons for Units 1–12 include all the words on the official USCIS writing vocabulary list. Even if students already have basic writing skills, they may benefit from this practice in order to assure that their formation of letters and their writing of words and sentences is legible and accurate. Lower-level students will find it helpful to complete a unit's tracing and copying practice before taking the unit test in the student book, which requires students to write sentences from dictation as on the USCIS exam.

READING PRACTICE

Reading Practice lessons provide a unique combination of reading and writing practice that prepares students for the reading portion of the USCIS exam. The first section of each lesson contains columns of words that appear on the official USCIS reading vocabulary list. Students should practice reading these words aloud. The second section of each lesson consists of sentences with blanks, which students complete by filling in the correct words from a choice-box. All the words students write are included on the official USCIS writing vocabulary list. And all the sentences that students complete in the lessons for Units 1–12 are plausible sentences that might occur in the reading portion of the USCIS exam. Therefore, after students fill in the sentences, they should practice reading the sentences aloud.

CIVICS PRACTICE

Civics Practice lessons offer practice with all the USCIS civics test content, including principles of American democracy, the system of government, rights and responsibilities, U.S. history, geography, national symbols, and holidays.

INTERVIEW PRACTICE

Interview Practice lessons support the English Speaking Test Prep section on pages 213–225 of the student book. This section prepares students to communicate successfully during all phases of their citizenship interview and exam—very important since the USCIS officer will evaluate the student's English speaking ability during the course of the interview. These lessons help students practice how to greet the officer, how to engage in small talk while walking to the interview room, and how to provide or verify personal information that appears on the citizenship application. This section also provides important practice with the challenging "Part 10" questions on the application form—the "Have you ever" questions that include difficult vocabulary and ask about sensitive subject matter such as criminal background, failure to pay taxes, and other issues that can jeopardize an application for citizenship.

The Interview Practice lessons can be used with the recommended units, or they can be used at a time that is more appropriate based on the scheduling of your students' USCIS interviews. The correlation key on page iv of this workbook indicates the recommended English Speaking Test Prep section pages and their supporting Interview Practice lessons. This information is also provided at the bottom of each Interview Practice page.

Flash Cards: The *Voices of Freedom* Flash Cards are 100 picture cards and accompanying word/sentence cards that highlight key vocabulary related to the USCIS interview. These include the actions involved in arriving at the office, checking in, being sworn in, and presenting identification. They also include the most important words and concepts related to the officer's questions concerning the applicant's Form N-400, including eligibility for citizenship, residence, family, employment, time outside the United States, and the challenging "Part 10" questions.

Some Flash Card pages contain two columns with pairs of matching pictures and words/sentences. Other pages contain three columns with trios of matching pictures, questions, and answers. Students can cut up the cards and use them in a variety of ways:

- With Flash Card pages containing two columns, students can glue each picture card and its accompanying word/sentence card back-to-back to create a set of flash cards for vocabulary practice. With Flash Card pages containing three columns, they can glue each picture card and its accompanying question card back-to-back, allowing them to practice the meaning of the questions and then answer them; or they can glue each question card and answer card back-to-back to create a set of flash cards with text only.

- With all Flash Card pages (containing two or three columns), the cards with pictures and text can be cut up in order to play various memory and matching games.

   Students can play individual games such as concentration by placing a set of cards face down and then turning over two (or three) cards at a time to try to match the cards.

   Students can play a classroom matching game, in which you distribute the cards randomly to different students who then walk around the classroom to find the classmate(s) with their matching card(s).

Matching Activities: Matching activities offer students practice matching pictures and words/ sentences, practice matching questions that have the same meaning (in order to recognize different ways the USCIS officer might ask a question), and practice matching questions and answers.

PRACTICE TESTS

Two practice tests are provided at the end of the workbook. Students can use these tests to assess their civics knowledge, English skills, and readiness for the USCIS exam. In each test, Part A contains sixteen of the 100 official USCIS civics questions. Part B contains questions about the student's

Form N-400 information that typically occur during the USCIS interview and serve as the basis for the officer's evaluation of English verbal skills. If time and resources allow for one-to-one administration of the tests, evaluate each student individually as the student answers the questions in Parts A and B orally. Alternatively, students can write answers to the questions. Part C requires a brief one-to-one administration to evaluate the student's ability to read the sentences aloud. Part D can be a whole-class dictation. (The script for the dictation section is included in the answer key.) Two tests are included, giving students the option of using one as a pre-test before the course and one as a post-test upon completion. A different set of pre/ post tests is provided in the Teacher's Guide for evaluation of students' prior knowledge and skills before instruction and their achievement of learning objectives at the end of the course.

A FINAL WORD: THE GOAL OF CIVICS EDUCATION

A century ago, the goal of citizenship education in so-called "Americanization" classes was to indoctrinate students with U.S. civics information in a way that often discredited their native countries and cultures. It was as though students had to renounce their backgrounds and heritages in order to acquire knowledge about their new country. Now we aspire to a nobler effort: to offer students the civics knowledge and the reading, writing, and interview skills they need to attain citizenship, to live full and productive lives, and to participate fully in the civic life of their communities and the country, and to do so through an educational program that recognizes and respects the diversity of cultures, histories, and experiences that our students bring to our classrooms . . . and the nation.

Bill Bliss

Voices of Freedom
Unit A Writing Practice

Trace and copy the alphabet.

Aa _____   Bb _____   Cc _____   Dd _____

Ee _____   Ff _____   Gg _____   Hh _____

Ii _____   Jj _____   Kk _____   Ll _____

Mm _____   Nn _____   Oo _____   Pp _____

Qq _____   Rr _____   Ss _____   Tt _____

Uu _____   Vv _____   Ww _____

Xx _____   Yy _____   Zz _____

Trace and copy the numbers.

0 _____   1 _____   2 _____   3 _____   4 _____

5 _____   6 _____   7 _____   8 _____   9 _____

10 _____   11 _____   12 _____   13 _____   14 _____

15 _____   16 _____   17 _____   18 _____   19 _____

A. Read these words.

a	the	what
is	for	last
in	name	first
of	city	state
be	want	citizen

B. Write the correct word. Then read the sentence.

be	for	first	is	United States

1. My name _____ Carlos Rivera.

2. My _____ name is Carlos.

3. I want to _____ a citizen.

4. I'm applying _____ citizenship.

5. California is in the _____.

citizen	first	is	of	state

6. What _____ do you live in?

7. Where _____ Los Angeles?

8. What's your _____ name?

9. What's the name _____ your city?

10. Do you want to be a _____?

VOICES *of* FREEDOM
Unit B Writing Practice

Trace and copy the months.

January _____ July _____

February _____ August _____

March _____ September _____

April _____ October _____

May _____ November _____

June _____ December _____

Trace and copy the dates.

May 25, 2011 _____ 05/25/2011 _____

June 3, 1987 _____ 06/03/1987 _____

October 1, 2007 _____ 10/01/2007 _____

July 4, 1776 _____ 07/04/1776 _____

VOICES of FREEDOM
Unit B Reading Practice

A. Read these words.

a	was	what
is	are	where
in	the	state
be	city	citizen
of	name	country

B. Write the correct word. Then read the sentence.

citizens	city	country	name	state

1. My _____ is Maria Lopez.

2. Houston is a _____ in Texas.

3. Texas is a _____.

4. My native _____ is Mexico.

5. My mother and father are _____.

are	citizens	country	first	is

6. What's your _____ name?

7. Where _____ you from?

8. What _____ your address?

9. What _____ are you from?

10. Are your mother and father _____ of the United States?

VOICES of FREEDOM
Unit 1 Writing Practice

Trace and copy the words.

has _____   Alaska _____

is _____   Canada _____

largest _____   capital _____

Mexico _____   New York City _____

most _____   people _____

north _____   south _____

of _____   United States _____

the _____   Washington, D.C. _____

Trace and copy the sentences.

Canada is north of the United States.

_____

Alaska is the largest state in the United States.

_____

The capital of the United States is Washington, D.C.

_____

VOICES of FREEDOM
Unit 1 Reading Practice

A. Read these words.

is	most	capital
of	what	country
has	north	largest
the	south	United States
city	people	

B. Write the correct word. Then read the sentence.

capital	has	largest	south	the

1. What country is _____ of the United States?

2. What is the _____ of the United States?

3. What is the _____ state in the United States?

4. What city _____ the most people?

5. What country is north of _____ United States?

is	north	of	people	state

6. What city in the United States has the most _____?

7. What is the capital _____ the United States?

8. What country _____ south of the United States?

9. What is the largest _____ in the United States?

10. What country is _____ of the United States?

Voices of Freedom
Unit 1 Civics Practice

A. Match the question and the correct answer.

_____ 1. What is the capital of the United States?

_____ 2. Where is the Statue of Liberty?

_____ 3. What ocean is on the East Coast of the United States?

_____ 4. What ocean is on the West Coast of the United States?

_____ 5. Name one state that borders Mexico.

_____ 6. Name one state that borders Canada.

_____ 7. Name one U.S. territory.

_____ 8. Name one of the two longest rivers in the United States.

a. The Atlantic Ocean

b. Puerto Rico

c. Ohio

d. The Missouri River

e. Washington, D.C.

f. The Pacific Ocean

g. Texas

h. New York Harbor

B. Match the words.

_____ 1. The Mississippi

_____ 2. The Pacific

_____ 3. The U.S. Virgin

_____ 4. New York

a. Islands

b. River

c. Harbor

d. Ocean

VOICES *of* FREEDOM
Unit 2 Writing Practice

Name _____

Date _____

Trace and copy the words.

and _____   Alaska _____

blue _____   California _____

flag _____   capital _____

has _____   fifty _____

is _____   50 _____

most _____   largest _____

of _____   people _____

red _____   United States _____

state _____   Washington, D.C. _____

the _____   white _____

Trace and copy the sentences.

The United States has fifty states.

_____

The flag is red, white, and blue.

_____

The state of California has the most people.

_____

VOICES of FREEDOM
Unit 2 Reading Practice

A. Read these words.

in	has	state	how many
is	have	colors	American flag
on	does	people	United States
are	most	country	Washington, D.C.
the	what	largest	

B. Write the correct word. Then read the sentence.

capital	flag	largest	people	states

1. What are the colors on the American _____?

2. How many _____ does the United States have?

3. What is the _____ state in the United States?

4. What is the _____ of the United States?

5. What state has the most _____ in the United States?

American	have	is	state	United States

6. What _____ Washington, D.C.?

7. What are the colors on the _____ flag?

8. How many states does the United States _____?

9. What _____ has the most people?

10. Where is the capital of the _____?

VOICES of FREEDOM
Unit 2 Civics Practice

A. Match the question and the correct answer.

____ 1. What are the colors on the American flag?

____ 2. Why does the flag have fifty stars?

____ 3. Why does the flag have thirteen stripes?

____ 4. What do we show loyalty to when we say the Pledge of Allegiance?

a. The flag

b. Red, white, and blue

c. Because there are fifty states

d. Because there were thirteen original colonies

B. Write the correct words. Then read the Pledge of Allegiance.

and	flag	for	one	to	United States

I pledge allegiance to the _____ [1]

of the _____ [2] of America,

and _____ [3] the republic

_____ [4] which it stands,

_____ [5] nation, under God,

indivisible, with liberty _____ [6] justice for all.

10

Voices of Freedom
Unit 3 Writing Practice

Trace and copy the words.

in _____   Congress _____

is _____   President _____

lives _____   Senators _____

meet _____   United States _____

meets _____   Washington, D.C. _____

of _____   White House _____

the _____

Trace and copy the sentences.

The President lives in the White House.

_____

The Congress meets in Washington, D.C.

_____

United States Senators meet in Washington, D.C.

_____

VOICES of FREEDOM
Unit 3 Reading Practice

A. Read these words.

do	who	Congress
in	does	Senators
is	meet	President
of	lives	White House
the	where	United States

B. Write the correct word. Then read the sentence.

capital	President	Senators	United States	White House

1. Who is the President of the _____?

2. Where do United States _____ meet?

3. Where does the _____ live?

4. Who lives in the _____?

5. What is the _____ of the United States?

lives	meet	of	the	Washington, D.C.

6. Who _____ in the White House?

7. Where does the Congress _____?

8. What is _____?

9. Who is _____ President of the United States?

10. What is the capital _____ the United States?

12

VOICES of FREEDOM
Unit 3 Civics Practice

A. Match the people and the correct branch of the government.

____ 1. The Supreme Court justices

____ 2. The President and the Vice President

____ 3. Senators and representatives

a. The executive branch

b. The legislative branch

c. The judicial branch

B. Write the correct word to complete the sentence.

checks	executive	judicial	legislative	President

1. The _____ branch makes the laws.

2. The _____ branch explains the laws.

3. The _____ branch enforces the laws.

4. A system of _____ and balances stops one branch of government from becoming too powerful.

5. The _____ is in charge of the executive branch.

C. Match the question and the correct answer.

____ 1. Name one branch of the government.

____ 2. Who is in charge of the executive branch?

____ 3. What stops one branch of government from becoming too powerful?

a. Separation of powers

b. The legislative branch

c. The President

Trace and copy the words.

can _____   citizens _____

elect _____   Congress _____

fifty _____   November _____

50 _____   one hundred _____

for _____   100 _____

has _____   people _____

in _____   President _____

of _____   Senators _____

the _____   states _____

vote _____   United States _____

Trace and copy the sentences.

Citizens vote in November.

_____

The Congress has 100 Senators.

_____

People vote for President in November.

_____

Voices of Freedom
Unit 4 Reading Practice

Name _____

Date _____

A. Read these words.

do	the	vote	Senators
in	who	elects	President
of	when	people	government
can	does	citizens	how many
for	have	Congress	United States

B. Write the correct word. Then read the sentence.

citizens	elects	Senators	United States	vote

1. Who elects the _____ Senators?

2. When do people in the United States _____ for the President?

3. How many _____ does the Congress have?

4. When do _____ vote for the government?

5. Who _____ the President?

Congress	elects	people	the	vote

6. Who can _____ for the President of the United States?

7. When do _____ in the United States vote for Congress?

8. How many Senators does the _____ have?

9. Who _____ the Congress of the United States?

10. When do citizens vote for _____ President?

Voices of Freedom
Unit 4 Civics Practice

Name _____

Date _____

A. Match the question and the correct answer.

_____ 1. What are the two parts of the U.S. Congress?

_____ 2. Who does a U.S. Senator represent?

_____ 3. Why do some states have more representatives than other states?

_____ 4. Who signs bills to become laws?

_____ 5. If the President can no longer serve, who becomes President?

_____ 6. What are two Cabinet-level positions?

a. All the people of the state

b. Attorney General and Secretary of Labor

c. The Vice President

d. Because of the state's population

e. The Senate and House

f. The President

B. Match the question and the correct answer.

_____ 1. Who makes federal laws?

_____ 2. Who is the Commander-in-Chief of the military?

_____ 3. What is the highest court in the United States?

_____ 4. In what month do we vote for President?

_____ 5. What does the President's Cabinet do?

_____ 6. What does the judicial branch do?

a. It advises the President.

b. The Supreme Court

c. It explains laws.

d. Congress

e. November

f. The President

C. Write the correct number to answer the question.

1. The House of Representatives has how many voting members? _____

2. We elect a U.S. representative for how many years? _____

3. We elect a President for how many years? _____

4. How many U.S. Senators are there? _____

5. We elect a U.S. Senator for how many years? _____

Trace and copy the words.

we _____   elect _____

for _____   citizens _____

have _____   Congress _____

in _____   November _____

lives _____   people _____

of _____   President _____

the _____   United States _____

vote _____   White House _____

freedom of speech _____

Trace and copy the sentences.

We vote for the President in November.

_____

Citizens of the United States elect the Congress.

_____

People in the United States have freedom of speech.

_____

A. Read these words.

do	the	what	people
in	who	when	Congress
is	does	where	President
of	live	right	United States
for	vote	elects	Bill of Rights
one			

B. Write the correct word. Then read the sentence.

elects	one	people	President	votes

1. When do _____ in the United States vote for the Congress?

2. Where does the _____ of the United States live?

3. Who _____ the President?

4. What is _____ right in the Bill of Rights?

5. Who _____ for the Congress?

citizens	Congress	in	of	votes	White House

6. Who _____ for the President of the United States?

7. How many Senators are in the _____?

8. When do _____ elect the Congress?

9. Who lives in the _____?

10. What is one right _____ the Bill _____ Rights?

Voices of Freedom
Unit 5 Civics Practice

Name _____

Date _____

Match the question and the correct answer.

_____ 1. What is the supreme law of the land?

_____ 2. What does the Constitution do?

_____ 3. What is the economic system in the United States?

_____ 4. What is an amendment?

_____ 5. What is one right or freedom from the First Amendment?

_____ 6. What is the "rule of law"?

_____ 7. What do we call the first ten amendments to the Constitution?

_____ 8. What is freedom of religion?

_____ 9. What is one power of the federal government?

_____ 10. What is one power of the states?

_____ 11. How many amendments does the Constitution have?

_____ 12. The idea of self-government is in the first three words of the Constitution. What are these words?

a. A capitalist economy

b. To print money

c. Everyone must follow the law.

d. It means you can practice any religion, or not practice a religion.

e. The Constitution

f. Twenty-seven

g. Freedom of speech

h. We the People

i. It sets up the government.

j. The Bill of Rights

k. To give a driver's license

l. A change to the Constitution

Trace and copy the words.

be	_____	want	_____
first	_____	was	_____
free	_____	October	_____
here	_____	November	_____
in	_____	people	_____
is	_____	Thanksgiving	_____
lived	_____	Columbus Day	_____
the	_____	American Indians	_____
to	_____		

Trace and copy the sentences.

Thanksgiving is in November.

_____

Columbus Day is in October.

_____

American Indians lived here first.

_____

VOICES of FREEDOM
Unit 6 Reading Practice

A. Read these words.

do	the	when	people
in	was	come	America
is	who	first	Columbus Day
to	why	lived	Thanksgiving

B. Write the correct word. Then read the sentence.

come	first	is	people	Thanksgiving

1. When is _____?

2. Why do _____ come to America?

3. Who lived in America _____?

4. When _____ Columbus Day?

5. When did you _____ to the United States?

Columbus Day	come	lived	want	was

6. When _____ the first Thanksgiving?

7. Why do people want to _____ here?

8. Who _____ in America first?

9. When is _____?

10. Do you _____ to be a citizen?

Voices of Freedom
Unit 6 Civics Practice

A. Match the question and the correct answer.

_____ 1. What is one reason colonists came to America?   **a.** October

_____ 2. Who lived in America before the Europeans arrived?   **b.** November

_____ 3. Name one American Indian tribe in the United States.   **c.** American Indians

_____ 4. When is Thanksgiving?   **d.** Religious freedom

_____ 5. When is Columbus Day?   **e.** Cherokee

B. Match the question and the correct answer.

_____ 1. Name one American Indian tribe in the United States.   **a.** Freedom

_____ 2. What is one reason colonists came to America?   **b.** Native Americans

_____ 3. Who lived in America before the Europeans arrived?   **c.** Navajo

C. Match the words that have the same meaning.

_____ 1. colonies   **a.** People who came to live in America

_____ 2. American Indians   **b.** Original thirteen states

_____ 3. colonists   **c.** Native Americans

D. Match the words to complete the reasons people came to America.

_____ 1. Practice their   **a.** opportunity

_____ 2. Economic   **b.** persecution

_____ 3. Escape   **c.** liberty

_____ 4. Political   **d.** religion

Trace and copy the words.

be _____

free _____

have _____

in _____

is _____

July _____

of _____

the _____

to _____

was _____

first _____

capital _____

people _____

President _____

right _____

United States _____

Washington _____

Washington, D.C. _____

Independence Day _____

Trace and copy the sentences.

Independence Day is in July.

_____

People have the right to be free.

_____

Washington was the first President of the United States.

_____

Voices of Freedom
Unit 7 Reading Practice

Name _____

Date _____

A. Read these words.

do	was	right	President
in	who	first	United States
is	what	people	Independence Day
of	when	capital	George Washington
the	have		

B. Write the correct word. Then read the sentence.

George Washington	is	President	right	United States

1. When _____ Independence Day?

2. Who was the first _____ of the United States?

3. What _____ do people in the United States have?

4. Who was _____?

5. What is the capital of the _____?

capital	have	Independence Day	President	was

6. Where does the _____ live?

7. Who _____ George Washington?

8. When is _____?

9. What right do people _____ in America?

10. What is the _____ of the United States?

Name _____

Date _____

A. Match the question and the correct answer.

_____ 1. Who wrote the Declaration of Independence?

_____ 2. When was the Declaration of Independence adopted?

_____ 3. Why did the colonists fight the British?

_____ 4. What did the Declaration of Independence do?

_____ 5. When do we celebrate Independence Day?

_____ 6. What are two rights in the Declaration of Independence?

a. Life and liberty

b. Thomas Jefferson

c. It announced our independence from Great Britain.

d. Because of high taxes

e. July 4

f. July 4, 1776

B. Match to complete the reasons the colonists fought the British.

_____ 1. Because they didn't have

_____ 2. Because of high

_____ 3. Because of boarding and quartering

_____ 4. Because of taxation without

_____ 5. Because the British army stayed in their

a. houses

b. the British army

c. taxes

d. self-government

e. representation

VOICES *of* FREEDOM
Unit 8 Writing Practice

Trace and copy the words.

first _____   capital _____

is _____   Delaware _____

of _____   dollar bill _____

on _____   President _____

state _____   Washington _____

the _____   United States _____

was _____   New York City _____

Father of Our Country _____

Trace and copy the sentences.

Delaware was the first state.

_____

The President on the dollar bill is Washington.

_____

The first United States capital was New York City.

_____

Voices of Freedom
Unit 8 Reading Practice

A. Read these words.

in	was	city	dollar bill
is	who	first	United States
of	why	state	George Washington
on	what	capital	Father of Our Country
the			

B. Write the correct word. Then read the sentence.

Father of Our Country	first	state	United States	was

1. What _____ one of the first states?

2. Who was the first President of the _____?

3. What city was the _____ capital of the country?

4. Who is the _____?

5. What was the first _____ in the United States?

capital	city	dollar bill	George Washington	President

6. Who was the first _____ of the United States?

7. What _____ was the first capital of the United States?

8. Who was _____?

9. Who is on the _____?

10. What is the _____ of the United States?

VOICES of FREEDOM
Unit 8 Civics Practice

Match the question and the correct answer.

_____ 1. Who is the *Father of Our Country?*

_____ 2. What is the supreme law of the land?

_____ 3. When was the Constitution written?

_____ 4. What is an amendment?

_____ 5. How many amendments does the Constitution have?

_____ 6. There were thirteen original states. Name three.

_____ 7. What happened at the Constitutional Convention?

_____ 8. What does the Constitution do?

_____ 9. What do we call the first ten amendments to the Constitution?

_____ 10. The Federalist Papers supported the passage of the U.S. Constitution. Name one of the writers.

_____ 11. What is one thing Benjamin Franklin is famous for?

_____ 12. What is one right or freedom from the First Amendment?

a. The Bill of Rights

b. 1787

c. New York, New Jersey, and Pennsylvania

d. George Washington

e. It defines the government.

f. He was a U.S. diplomat.

g. The Constitution

h. James Madison

i. 27

j. Freedom of the press

k. The Constitution was written.

l. A change to the Constitution

Trace and copy the words.

can _____

have _____

one _____

was _____

vote _____

right _____

state _____

people _____

Alaska _____

freedom of speech _____

during _____

citizens _____

Civil War _____

February _____

largest _____

President _____

Presidents' Day _____

United States _____

Abraham Lincoln _____

Trace and copy the sentences.

Presidents' Day is in February.

_____

Alaska is the largest state in the United States.

_____

Abraham Lincoln was President during the Civil War.

_____

Voices of Freedom
Unit 9 Reading Practice

A. Read these words.

in	the	vote	Bill of Rights
is	was	right	United States
can	who	state	Presidents' Day
for	what	largest	Abraham Lincoln
one	when	President	

B. Write the correct word. Then read the sentence.

is	President	right	state	vote

1. When _____ Presidents' Day?

2. What is one _____ people have?

3. When was Abraham Lincoln the _____?

4. What is the largest _____ in the country?

5. Who can citizens _____ for?

Abraham Lincoln	citizen	have	largest	Presidents' Day

6. What is the _____ state in the United States?

7. What right do people in the United States _____?

8. When is _____?

9. When can a _____ vote for President?

10. When was _____ the President?

VOICES of FREEDOM
Unit 9 Civics Practice

Match the question and the correct answer.

_____ 1. What is an amendment?

_____ 2. How many amendments does the Constitution have?

_____ 3. How old do citizens have to be to vote for President?

_____ 4. What is the name of the national anthem?

_____ 5. What group of people was taken to America and sold as slaves?

_____ 6. Name the U.S. war between the North and the South.

_____ 7. What do we call the first ten amendments to the Constitution?

_____ 8. Name one problem that led to the Civil War.

_____ 9. What territory did the United States buy from France in 1803?

_____ 10. What did the Emancipation Proclamation do?

_____ 11. What was one important thing that Abraham Lincoln did?

_____ 12. What is one right or freedom from the First Amendment?

_____ 13. What did Susan B. Anthony do?

_____ 14. There are four amendments to the Constitution about who can vote. Describe one of them.

a. The Bill of Rights

b. 18 and older

c. The Louisiana Territory

d. She fought for women's rights.

e. He saved the Union.

f. People from Africa

g. It freed the slaves.

h. An addition to the Constitution

i. Freedom of assembly

j. Any citizen can vote.

k. The Civil War

l. The *Star-Spangled Banner*

m. States' rights

n. 27

Trace and copy the words.

and _____   have _____

be _____   vote _____

can _____   citizens _____

come _____   Labor Day _____

for _____   people _____

free _____   President _____

to _____   Senators _____

of _____   September _____

the _____   United States _____

freedom of speech _____

Trace and copy the sentences.

Labor Day is in September.

_____

People in the United States have freedom of speech.

_____

Citizens can vote for the President of the United States.

_____

Voices of Freedom
Unit 10 Reading Practice

Name _____

Date _____

A. Read these words.

do	for	when	right
in	one	come	people
is	the	have	citizens
of	who	name	Labor Day
to	why	vote	United States
can	what		

B. Write the correct word. Then read the sentence.

citizens	come	is	right	vote

1. When _____ Labor Day?

2. Why do people _____ to the United States?

3. Who can _____ of the United States vote for?

4. Name one _____ people have in the United States.

5. When do we _____ for the Congress?

Labor Day	Name	people	United States	vote

6. What is one right _____ have?

7. Who can _____ for President?

8. _____ the first President of the United States.

9. When is _____?

10. What can citizens of the _____ do?

33

Voices of Freedom
Unit 10 Civics Practice

A. Match the question and the correct answer.

_____ 1. Who was President during the Great Depression?

_____ 2. What did Martin Luther King, Jr., do?

_____ 3. Name one war fought by the United States in the 1900s.

_____ 4. During the Cold War, what was the main concern of the United States?

_____ 5. Who was President during World War I?

_____ 6. Who did the United States fight in World War II?

a. Communism

b. The Vietnam War

c. Japan, Germany, and Italy

d. He fought for civil rights.

e. Woodrow Wilson

f. Franklin Roosevelt

B. Match the question and the correct answer.

_____ 1. Before he was President, Eisenhower was a general. What war was he in?

_____ 2. What movement tried to end racial discrimination?

_____ 3. Who was President during World War II?

_____ 4. What did Martin Luther King, Jr., do?

_____ 5. What major event happened on September 11, 2001, in the United States?

a. The civil rights movement

b. He worked for equality for all Americans.

c. World War II

d. Terrorists attacked the United States.

e. Franklin Roosevelt

Trace and copy the words.

February _____   Presidents' Day _____

May _____   Memorial Day _____

June _____   Flag Day _____

July _____   Independence Day _____

September _____   Labor Day _____

October _____   Columbus Day _____

November _____   Thanksgiving _____

Trace and copy the sentences.

Flag Day is in June.

_____

Memorial Day is in May.

_____

Columbus Day is in October.

_____

Thanksgiving is in November.

_____

Independence Day is in July.

_____

Voices of Freedom
Unit 11 Reading Practice

Name _____

Date _____

A. Read these words.

in	July	September	Memorial Day
is	October	Flag Day	Columbus Day
when	November	Labor Day	Presidents' Day
May	February	Thanksgiving	Independence Day
June			

B. Write the correct word. Then read the sentence.

is	Labor Day	lives	Memorial	President

1. When _____ Thanksgiving?

2. When is _____ Day?

3. When is _____?

4. Who was the first _____ of the United States?

5. Who _____ in the White House?

Independence	is	of	Presidents' Day	Washington

6. When _____ Flag Day?

7. When is _____ Day?

8. When is _____?

9. Who is the Father _____ Our Country?

10. Who was George _____?

Match the question and the correct answer.

____ 1. Who was the first President?

____ 2. What are the two major political parties in the United States?

____ 3. When do we celebrate Independence Day?

____ 4. Who wrote the Declaration of Independence?

____ 5. The Federalist Papers supported the passage of the U.S. Constitution. Name one of the writers.

____ 6. Who was President during World War I?

____ 7. Before he was President, Eisenhower was a general. What war was he in?

____ 8. What did the Emancipation Proclamation do?

____ 9. What was one important thing that Abraham Lincoln did?

____ 10. Name two national U.S. holidays.

____ 11. What territory did the United States buy from France in 1803?

____ 12. What major event happened on September 11, 2001, in the United States?

____ 13. Who was President during World War II?

a. Alexander Hamilton

b. It freed slaves in most Southern states.

c. World War II

d. George Washington

e. Louisiana

f. Memorial Day and Veterans Day

g. Franklin Roosevelt

h. Terrorists attacked the United States.

i. Democratic and Republican

j. Woodrow Wilson

k. Thomas Jefferson

l. He preserved the Union.

m. July 4

Trace and copy the words.

and _____

citizens _____

can _____

Congress _____

for _____

elect _____

have _____

people _____

in _____

President _____

of _____

right _____

pay _____

taxes _____

the _____

United States _____

to _____

vote _____

Trace and copy the sentences.

People in the United States have to pay taxes.

_____

Citizens of the United States elect the President.

_____

Citizens can vote for the President and the Congress.

_____

VOICES of FREEDOM
Unit 12 Reading Practice

Name _____

Date _____

A. Read these words.

do	for	what	people
in	one	have	citizens
is	pay	vote	President
of	the	right	government
to	who	elects	United States
can			

B. Write the correct word. Then read the sentence.

citizens	pay	President	right	vote

1. When do we _____ for the Congress?

2. Who can _____ vote for?

3. Who elects the _____ of the United States?

4. Who has the _____ to vote?

5. Why do people in the United States have to _____ taxes?

can	elect	have	taxes	vote

6. When do citizens _____ the President?

7. Who _____ vote for the President?

8. Who has to pay _____?

9. When do citizens _____ for the Congress?

10. What do people _____ to pay to the government?

VOICES of FREEDOM
Unit 12 Civics Practice

A. Match the question and the correct answer.

____ 1. How old do citizens have to be to vote for President?

____ 2. What are two rights of everyone living in the United States?

____ 3. What are the two major political parties in the United States?

____ 4. Name one right only for United States citizens.

____ 5. What is one responsibility that is only for United States citizens?

____ 6. What are two ways that Americans can participate in their democracy?

a. Democratic and Republican

b. Join a civic group and give an elected official your opinion on an issue.

c. Serve on a jury.

d. 18 and older

e. Freedom of expression and the right to bear arms

f. The right to vote in a federal election

B. Match the question and the correct answer.

____ 1. Name one right only for United States citizens.

____ 2. When is the last day you can send in federal income tax forms?

____ 3. When must all men register for the Selective Service?

____ 4. What is one promise you make when you become a United States citizen?

____ 5. What are two rights of everyone living in the United States?

a. April 15

b. Freedom of speech and freedom of worship

c. The right to run for federal office

d. At age 18

e. Give up loyalty to other countries.

Show your appointment letter to the security guard.

Put your bag on the conveyor belt.

Put any metal objects in the tray.

Step through the metal detector.

Check in at the reception counter.

Take a seat in the waiting area.

Interview Practice 2: Matching

Name _____

Date _____

Match the picture and the correct sentence.

_____ 1.

a. Put any metal objects in the tray.

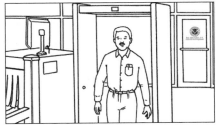

_____ 2.

b. Take a seat in the waiting area.

_____ 3.

c. Check in at the reception counter.

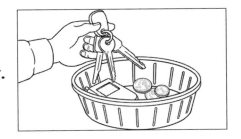

_____ 4.

d. Step through the metal detector.

_____ 5.

e. Show your appointment letter to the security guard.

_____ 6.

f. Put your bag on the conveyor belt.

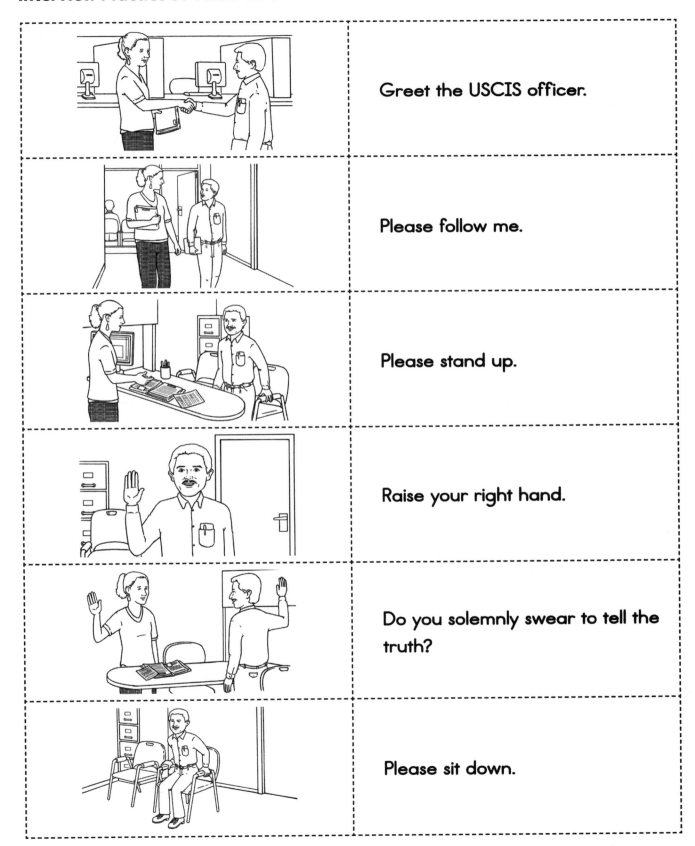

Greet the USCIS officer.

Please follow me.

Please stand up.

Raise your right hand.

Do you solemnly swear to tell the truth?

Please sit down.

Voices of Freedom
Interview Practice 4: Matching

Match the picture and the correct sentence.

_____ 1.

a. Please stand up.

_____ 2.

b. Please sit down.

_____ 3.

c. Please follow me.

_____ 4.

d. Greet the USCIS officer.

_____ 5.

e. Raise your right hand.

_____ 6.

f. Do you solemnly swear to tell the truth?

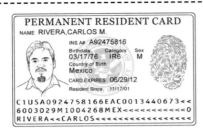

Please show me your permanent resident card.

Please show me your passport.

Please show me your driver's license.

Please show me your state identification card.

Do you have two passport-size photographs?

VOICES of FREEDOM
Interview Practice 6: Matching

Match the picture and the correct sentence.

_____ 1.

_____ 2.

_____ 3.

_____ 4.

_____ 5.

a. Please show me your passport.

b. Do you have two passport-size photographs?

c. Please show me your permanent resident card.

d. Please show me your state identification card.

e. Please show me your driver's license.

Carlos Manuel **Rivera**	**What's your family name?*** (*last name / surname)
Carlos Manuel Rivera	**What's your first name?*** (*given name)
Carlos **Manuel** Rivera	**What's your middle name?**
Carlos Manuel Rivera	**What's your full name?**
Carlos Manuel Rivera	**Print your name.**
Carlos M. Rivera SIGNATURE	**Sign your name.**

VOICES *of* FREEDOM

Interview Practice 8: Matching

Match the picture and the correct sentence.

_____ 1. | Carlos Manuel Rivera |

a. What's your family name?

_____ 2. | Carlos *Manuel Rivera* |

b. Sign your name.

_____ 3. | *Carlos Manuel* **Rivera** |

c. What's your full name?

_____ 4. | Carlos Manuel Rivera |

d. What's your middle name?

_____ 5. | *Carlos* **Manuel** *Rivera* |

e. What's your first name?

_____ 6. | Carlos M. Rivera
SIGNATURE |

f. Print your name.

Voices of Freedom
Interview Practice 9: Flash Cards

	husband
	wife
	father
	mother
	son
	daughter

VOICES of FREEDOM
Interview Practice 10: Matching

Match the picture and the correct word.

_____ 1.    **a.** son

_____ 2.    **b.** mother

_____ 3.    **c.** husband

_____ 4.    **d.** daughter

_____ 5.    **e.** father

_____ 6.    **f.** wife

VOICES of FREEDOM
Interview Practice 11: Flash Cards

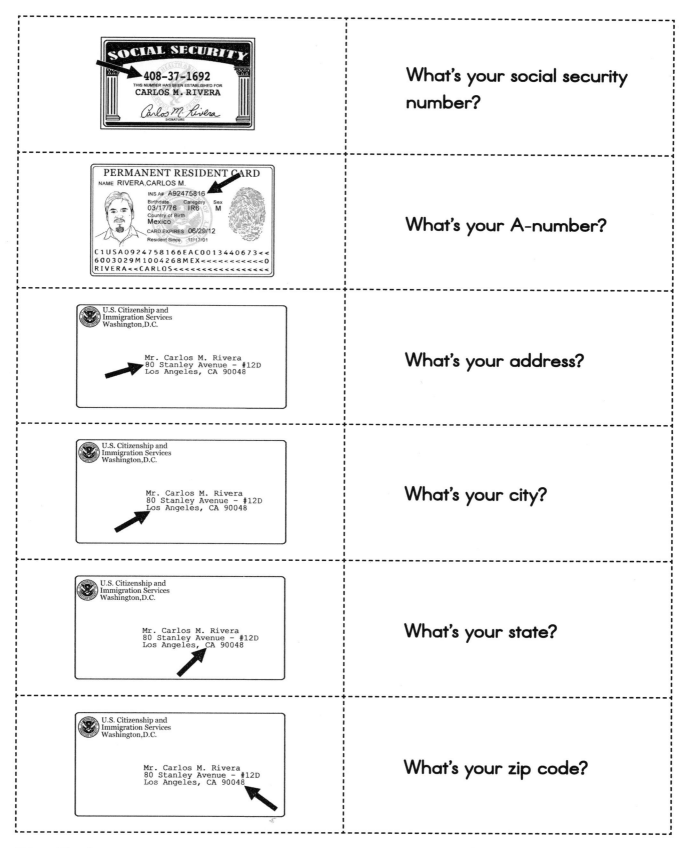

What's your social security number?

What's your A-number?

What's your address?

What's your city?

What's your state?

What's your zip code?

Voices of Freedom

Interview Practice 12: Matching

Match the picture and the correct question. Then answer the question with your own information.

_____ 1.

a. What's your social security number?

_____ 2.

b. What's your A-number?

_____ 3.

c. What's your city?

_____ 4.

d. What's your address?

_____ 5.

e. What's your state?

_____ 6.

f. What's your zip code?

Voices of Freedom
Interview Practice 13: Flash Cards

RIVERA **Carlos M** 80 Stanley Av
Los Angeles 213 257-9108

What's your phone number?

From: ascis@dhs.gov
Date: Tuesday, June 16, 2009
To: **cmrivera1976@ail.com**
Subject: Application

What's your email address?

05 / 04 / 1979

What's your date of birth?*

(*birth date)

May

05/ 04 /1979

In what month were you born?

1979

05/ 04 /1979

In what year were you born?

Match the picture and the correct question. Then answer the question with your own information.

_____ 1.

a. In what year were you born?

_____ 2.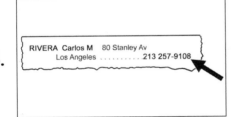

b. What's your email address?

_____ 3.

c. In what month were you born?

_____ 4.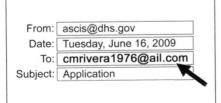

d. What's your date of birth?

_____ 5.

From: ascis@dhs.gov
Date: Tuesday, June 16, 2009
To: cmrivera1976@ail.com
Subject: Application

e. What's your phone number?

Voices of Freedom
Interview Practice 15: Flash Cards

Mexico	**What's your country of birth?*** (*Where were you born?)
Mexican	**What's your nationality?*** (*What's your country of nationality?)
	Are you single?
	Are you married?
	Are you divorced?
	Are you widowed?

Match the picture and the correct question. Then answer the question with your own information.

_____ 1.

a. Are you divorced?

_____ 2.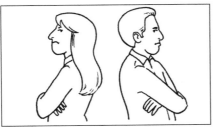

b. Are you widowed?

_____ 3.

c. Are you married?

_____ 4.

d. Are you single?

_____ 5.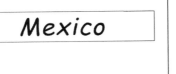

e. What's your nationality?

_____ 6.

f. What's your country of birth?

Voices of Freedom
Interview Practice 17: Flash Cards

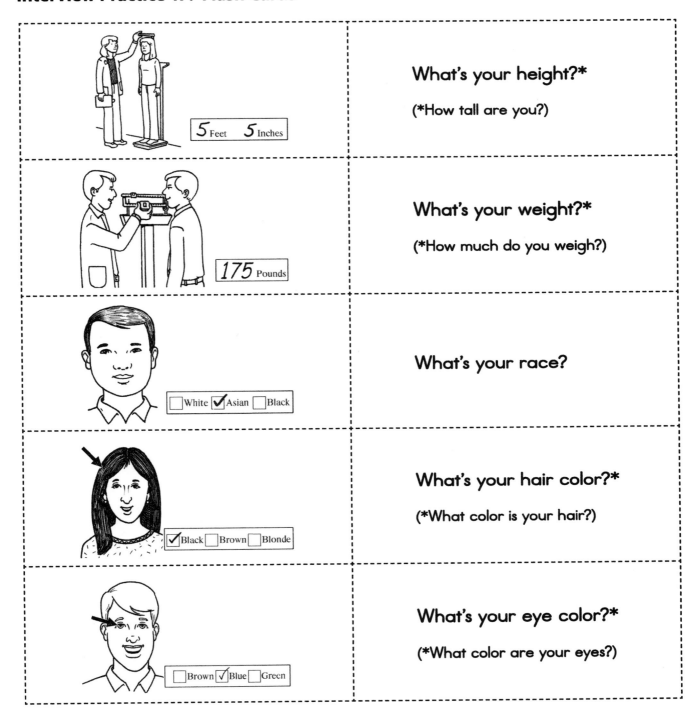

5 Feet   5 Inches

What's your height?*

(*How tall are you?)

175 Pounds

What's your weight?*

(*How much do you weigh?)

☐ White ☑ Asian ☐ Black

What's your race?

☑ Black ☐ Brown ☐ Blonde

What's your hair color?*

(*What color is your hair?)

☐ Brown ☑ Blue ☐ Green

What's your eye color?*

(*What color are your eyes?)

Name _____

Date _____

Match the picture and the correct question. Then answer the question with your own information.

_____ 1.

a. What's your race?

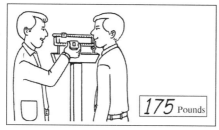

_____ 2.

b. What color are your eyes?

_____ 3.

c. What's your weight?

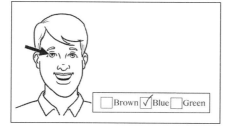

_____ 4.

d. How tall are you?

_____ 5.

e. What's your hair color?

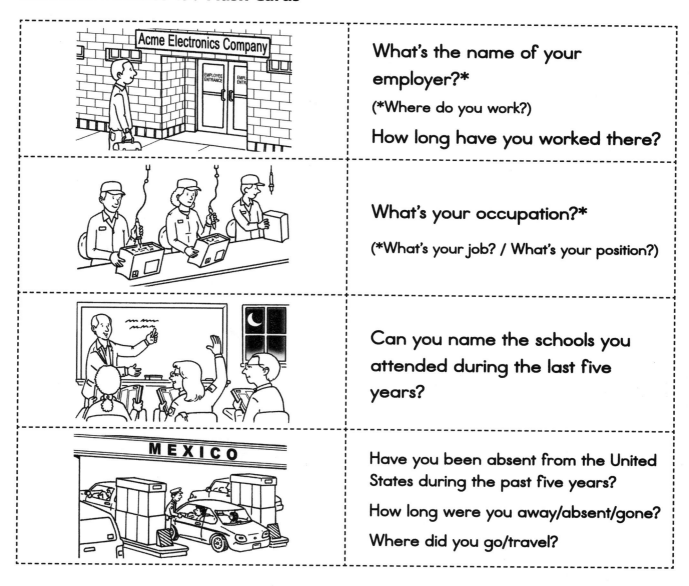

What's the name of your employer?*

(*Where do you work?)

How long have you worked there?

What's your occupation?*

(*What's your job? / What's your position?)

Can you name the schools you attended during the last five years?

Have you been absent from the United States during the past five years?

How long were you away/absent/gone?

Where did you go/travel?

VOICES of FREEDOM
Interview Practice 20: Matching

Match the picture and the correct question. Then answer the question with your own information.

_____ 1.

a. What's your occupation?

_____ 2.

b. What's the name of your employer?

_____ 3.

c. Can you name the schools you attended during the last five years?

_____ 4.

d. Have you been absent from the United States during the past five years?

Voices of Freedom

Interview Practice 21: Matching

Name _____

Date _____

Match the questions that have the same meaning. Then answer the questions.

_____ 1. Are you employed?

_____ 2. What's your position?

_____ 3. What was your previous address?

_____ 4. When was your most recent trip outside the United States?

_____ 5. Have you been absent from the United States during the past five years?

_____ 6. What was the reason for the trip?

_____ 7. How long were you away?

a. Why did you travel?

b. What's your occupation?

c. Where did you live before where you live now?

d. Have you spent time outside the United States during the past five years?

e. When did you last leave the country?

f. How long were you absent?

g. Do you work now?

Name _____

Date _____

Match the questions that have the same meaning.

_____ 1. Do you understand?

    a. How many children have you had?

_____ 2. Are you currently married?

    b. What's your current address?

_____ 3. When were you married?

    c. Could you please ask that again using different words?

_____ 4. Where do you live?

    d. Should I explain that for you?

_____ 5. Could you please say the question another way?

    e. Do you have a spouse?

_____ 6. Would you like me to explain that?

    f. What are their dates of birth?

_____ 7. How many children do you have?

    g. Do you know what that means?

_____ 8. When were they born?

    h. What's the date of your marriage?

VOICES of FREEDOM
Interview Practice 23: Flash Cards

Have you ever claimed to be a U.S. citizen?

No. I've never told anyone I am a U.S. citizen.

Have you ever registered to vote in any federal, state, or local election in the United States?

No. I've never registered to vote in this country. I want to be a citizen so I can vote in the future.

Have you ever voted in any federal, state, or local election in the United States?

No. I've never voted in an election. I want to be a citizen so I can vote in the future.

Since becoming a lawful permanent resident, have you ever failed to file a required federal, state, or local tax return?

No. I always send in all the required tax forms.

Do you owe any federal, state, or local taxes that are overdue?

No. I always pay my taxes on time.

Do you have any title of nobility in any foreign country?

No. I was just a regular person in my country—not a prince/princess or anything like that.

Voices of Freedom
Interview Practice 24: Matching

Match the question and the correct answer.

_____ 1. Have you ever voted in any federal, state, or local election in the United States?

a. No. I always pay my taxes on time.

_____ 2. Do you owe any federal, state, or local taxes that are overdue?

b. No. I've never registered to vote in this country. I want to be a citizen so I can vote in the future.

_____ 3. Do you have any title of nobility in any foreign country?

c. No. I always send in all the required tax forms.

_____ 4. Have you ever registered to vote in any federal, state, or local election in the United States?

d. No. I've never told anyone I am a U.S. citizen.

_____ 5. Have you ever claimed to be a U.S. citizen?

e. No. I've never voted in an election. I want to be a citizen so I can vote in the future.

_____ 6. Since becoming a lawful permanent resident, have you ever failed to file a required federal, state, or local tax return?

f. No. I was just a regular person in my country—not a prince / princess or anything like that.

Name _____

Date _____

Match the picture and the correct question. Then answer the question with your own information.

_____ 1.

a. Have you ever registered to vote in any federal, state, or local election in the United States?

_____ 2.

b. Have you ever claimed to be a U.S. citizen?

_____ 3.

c. Do you have any title of nobility in any foreign country?

_____ 4.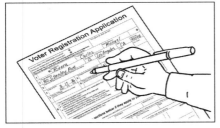

d. Do you owe any federal, state, or local taxes that are overdue?

_____ 5.

e. Have you ever voted in any federal, state, or local election in the United States?

_____ 6.

f. Since becoming a lawful permanent resident, have you ever failed to file a required federal, state, or local tax return?

	Have you ever been declared legally incompetent or been confined to a mental institution within the last five years?	No. I've never had mental health problems.
AMERICAN IMMIGRANT ASSOCIATION	Have you ever been a member of or associated with any organization, association, fund, foundation, party, club, society, or similar group in the United States or in any other place?	Yes. I'm a member of the parents' association in my children's school.
	Have you ever been a member of or in any way associated with the Communist Party?	No. I am not a Communist, and I never was a Communist. I don't believe in Communism.
	Have you ever been a member of or in any way associated with any other totalitarian party?	No. I believe that dictators are bad and that people in all countries should have rights and freedoms.
	Have you ever been a member of or in any way associated with a terrorist organization?	No. I believe that terrorism is very bad.
	Have you ever advocated the overthrow of any government by force or violence?	No. I think violence is bad. I believe that government should change peacefully through elections.

Voices of Freedom
Interview Practice 27: Matching

Name _____

Date _____

Match the question and the correct answer.

_____ 1. Have you ever been a member of or in any way associated with the Communist Party?

_____ 2. Have you ever been declared legally incompetent or been confined to a mental institution within the last five years?

_____ 3. Have you ever been a member of or in any way associated with a terrorist organization?

_____ 4. Have you ever advocated the overthrow of any government by force or violence?

_____ 5. Have you ever been a member of or in any way associated with any other totalitarian party?

_____ 6. Have you ever been a member of or associated with any organization, association, fund, foundation, party, club, society, or similar group in the United States or in any other place?

a. No. I believe that terrorism is very bad.

b. No. I believe that dictators are bad and that people in all countries should have rights and freedoms.

c. Yes. I'm a member of the parents' association in my children's school.

d. No. I've never had mental health problems.

e. No. I am not a Communist, and I never was a Communist. I don't believe in Communism.

f. No. I think violence is bad. I believe that government should change peacefully through elections.

VOICES of FREEDOM
Interview Practice 28: Matching

**Match the picture and the correct question. Then answer the question
with your own information.**

_____ 1.

_____ 2.

_____ 3.

_____ 4.

_____ 5.

_____ 6.

a. Have you ever been declared legally incompetent or been confined to a mental institution within the last five years?

b. Have you ever been a member of or associated with any organization, association, fund, foundation, party, club, society, or similar group in the United States or in any other place?

c. Have you ever been a member of or in any way associated with a terrorist organization?

d. Have you ever been a member of or in any way associated with any other totalitarian party?

e. Have you ever been a member of or in any way associated with the Communist Party?

f. Have you ever advocated the overthrow of any government by force or violence?

	Have you ever persecuted any person because of race, religion, national origin, membership in a particular social group, or political opinion?	No. I've never hurt any person in this way. I believe that people of all races, religions, and groups should have the same rights.
	Between March 23, 1933, and May 8, 1945, did you work for or associate in any way with the Nazi government of Germany?	No. I was never a Nazi. I had no connection with that government.
	Have you ever called yourself a "nonresident" on a federal, state, or local tax return?	No. When I file my tax returns, I file as a resident.
	Have you ever failed to file a federal, state, or local tax return because you considered yourself to be a nonresident?	No. I have always sent in all required tax forms.
	Have you ever committed a crime or offense for which you were not arrested?	No. I've never done anything that is against the law.
	Have you ever been arrested, cited, or detained by any law enforcement officer for any reason?	No. I've never had a problem with a police officer or other officer. Yes. _____* (*A police officer game me a ticket for _____. / I was arrested for _____.)

Name _____

Date _____

Match the question and the correct answer.

_____ 1. Have you ever called yourself a "nonresident" on a federal, state, or local tax return?

_____ 2. Have you ever committed a crime or offense for which you were not arrested?

_____ 3. Between March 23, 1933, and May 8, 1945, did you work for or associate in any way with the Nazi government of Germany?

_____ 4. Have you ever failed to file a federal, state, or local tax return because you considered yourself to be a nonresident?

_____ 5. Have you ever been arrested, cited, or detained by any law enforcement officer for any reason?

_____ 6. Have you ever persecuted any person because of race, religion, national origin, membership in a particular social group, or political opinion?

a. No. I was never a Nazi. I had no connection with that government.

b. No. I've never hurt any person in this way. I believe that people of all races, religions, and groups should have the same rights.

c. Yes. A police officer gave me a ticket for not wearing my seat belt while driving.

d. No. When I file my tax returns, I file as a resident.

e. No. I have always sent in all required tax forms.

f. No. I've never done anything that is against the law.

Name _____

Date _____

Match the picture and the correct question. Then answer the question with your own information.

_____ 1.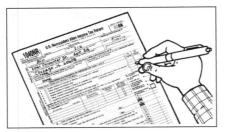

_____ 2.

_____ 3.

_____ 4.

_____ 5.

_____ 6.

a. Between March 23, 1933, and May 8, 1945, did you work for or associate in any way with the Nazi government of Germany?

b. Have you ever failed to file a federal, state, or local tax return because you considered yourself to be a nonresident?

c. Have you ever called yourself a "nonresident" on a federal, state, or local tax return?

d. Have you ever persecuted any person because of race, religion, national origin, membership in a particular social group, or political opinion?

e. Have you ever been arrested, cited, or detained by any law enforcement officer for any reason?

f. Have you ever committed a crime or offense for which you were not arrested?

	Have you ever been charged with committing any crime or offense?	No. I've never been accused of doing anything against the law.
	Have you ever been convicted of a crime or offense?	No. I've never been found guilty of doing anything against the law.
	Have you ever been placed in an alternative sentencing or a rehabilitative program?	No. I've never done anything against the law, so I've never been placed in a program like this.
	Have you ever received a suspended sentence?	No. I've never done anything against the law, so I've never received a suspended sentence.
	Have you ever been placed on probation?	No. I've never done anything against the law, so I've never been placed on probation.
	Have you ever been paroled?	No. I've never done anything against the law, so I've never been paroled.

Match the question and the correct answer.

_____ 1. Have you ever been charged with committing any crime or offense?

a. No. I've never done anything against the law, so I've never received a suspended sentence.

_____ 2. Have you ever been convicted of a crime or offense?

b. No. I've never done anything against the law, so I've never been placed in a program like this.

_____ 3. Have you ever received a suspended sentence?

c. No. I've never done anything against the law, so I've never been paroled.

_____ 4. Have you ever been placed on probation?

d. No. I've never been found guilty of doing anything against the law.

_____ 5. Have you ever been paroled?

e. No. I've never been accused of doing anything against the law.

_____ 6. Have you ever been placed in an alternative sentencing or a rehabilitative program?

f. No. I've never done anything against the law, so I've never been placed on probation.

Match the picture and the correct question. Then answer the question with your own information.

_____ 1.

a. Have you ever been charged with committing any crime or offense?

_____ 2.

b. Have you ever been convicted of a crime or offense?

_____ 3.

c. Have you ever been placed on probation?

_____ 4.

d. Have you ever been placed in an alternative sentencing or a rehabilitative program?

_____ 5.

e. Have you ever been paroled?

_____ 6.

f. Have you ever received a suspended sentence?

Have you ever been in jail or prison?

No. I've never been found guilty of anything, so I've never been in jail or prison.

Have you ever been a habitual drunkard?

No. I don't drink alcohol.

No. I rarely drink alcohol.

Have you ever been a prostitute, or procured anyone for prostitution?

No. I've never sold my body or paid for sex.

Have you ever sold or smuggled controlled substances, illegal drugs, or narcotics?

No. I've never sold any illegal drugs or brought them into the country.

Have you ever been married to more than one person at the same time?

No. I've never had more than one wife/husband at a time.

No. I've never been married to anyone.

Have you ever helped anyone enter or try to enter the United States illegally?

No. I've never helped anyone come into the country without permission.

Voices of Freedom
Interview Practice 36: Matching

Match the question and the correct answer.

_____ 1. Have you ever been a habitual drunkard?

a. No. I've never been found guilty of anything, so I've never been in jail or prison.

_____ 2. Have you ever helped anyone enter or try to enter the United States illegally?

b. No. I've never had more than one wife/husband at a time.

_____ 3. Have you ever been in jail or prison?

c. No. I don't drink alcohol.

_____ 4. Have you ever sold or smuggled controlled substances, illegal drugs, or narcotics?

d. No. I've never sold my body or paid for sex.

_____ 5. Have you ever been married to more than one person at the same time?

e. No. I've never helped anyone come into the country without permission.

_____ 6. Have you ever been a prostitute, or procured anyone for prostitution?

f. No. I've never sold any illegal drugs or brought them into the country.

Voices *of* Freedom

Interview Practice 37: Matching

Match the picture and the correct question. Then answer the question with your own information.

_____ 1.

a. Have you ever helped anyone enter or try to enter the United States illegally?

_____ 2.

b. Have you ever been in jail or prison?

_____ 3.

c. Have you ever been a habitual drunkard?

_____ 4.

d. Have you ever been married to more than one person at the same time?

_____ 5.

e. Have you ever sold or smuggled controlled substances, illegal drugs, or narcotics?

_____ 6.

f. Have you ever been a prostitute, or procured anyone for prostitution?

Voices of Freedom

Interview Practice 39: Matching

Match the question and the correct answer.

_____ 1. Have you ever failed to support your dependents or pay alimony?

_____ 2. Have you ever lied to any U.S. government official to gain entry or admission into the United States?

_____ 3. Have you ever gambled illegally or received income from illegal gambling?

_____ 4. Have you ever been removed, excluded, or deported from the United States?

_____ 5. Have you ever given false or misleading information to any U.S. government official while applying for any immigration benefit or to prevent deportation, exclusion, or removal?

a. No. I've never gambled money in a way that's against the law.

b. No. I have never been ordered to leave the United States.

c. No. I always provide money to my children and former wife.

d. No. I have never lied while applying for any immigration benefit or to prevent being ordered to leave the United States.

e. No. I have always told the truth when entering the United States.

Match the picture and the correct question. Then answer the question with your own information.

_____ 1.

a. Have you ever lied to any U.S. government official to gain entry or admission into the United States?

_____ 2.

b. Have you ever gambled illegally or received income from illegal gambling?

_____ 3.

c. Have you ever been removed, excluded, or deported from the United States?

_____ 4.

d. Have you ever given false or misleading information to any U.S. government official while applying for any immigration benefit or to prevent deportation, exclusion, or removal?

_____ 5.

e. Have you ever failed to support your dependents or pay alimony?

VOICES of FREEDOM
Interview Practice 41: Flash Cards

	Have you ever served in the U.S. Armed Forces?	Yes. I have served in the U.S. military. No. I haven't served in the U.S. military.
	Have you ever left the United States to avoid being drafted into the U.S. Armed Forces?	No. I have never left the country to avoid military service.
	Have you ever applied for any kind of exemption from military service in the U.S. Armed Forces?	No. I have never asked to be excused from military service.
	Have you ever deserted from the U.S. Armed Forces?	No. I never ran away during my military service.
	Have you registered with the Selective Service System?	Yes. I registered for military service _____.* (*online / at the post office / at my high school) No. I wasn't a resident of the United States when I was between the ages of 18 and 26.

Voices of Freedom

Interview Practice 42: Matching

Match the question and the correct answer.

_____ 1. Have you registered with the Selective Service System?

    a. No. I have never asked to be excused from military service.

_____ 2. Have you ever served in the U.S. Armed Forces?

    b. No. I have never left the country to avoid military service.

_____ 3. Have you ever applied for any kind of exemption from military service in the U.S. Armed Forces?

    c. Yes. I have served in the U.S. military.

_____ 4. Have you ever deserted from the U.S. Armed Forces?

    d. Yes. I registered for military service at the post office.

_____ 5. Have you ever left the United States to avoid being drafted into the U.S. Armed Forces?

    e. No. I never ran away during my military service.

Voices *of* Freedom
Interview Practice 43: Matching

Name _____

Date _____

Match the picture and the correct question. Then answer the question with your own information.

_____ 1.

a. Have you ever deserted from the U.S. Armed Forces?

_____ 2.

b. Have you ever left the United States to avoid being drafted into the U.S. Armed Forces?

_____ 3.

c. Have you ever applied for any kind of exemption from military service in the U.S. Armed Forces?

_____ 4.

d. Have you ever served in the U.S. Armed Forces?

_____ 5.

e. Have you registered with the Selective Service System?

	Do you support the Constitution and form of government of the United States?	Yes. I believe in the Constitution as the supreme law of the land, and I believe in our form of government.
	Are you willing to take the full Oath of Allegiance to the United States?	Yes. I am ready to promise to be loyal only to the United States, to support the Constitution and U.S. laws, and to fight or work for the United States if needed.
	If the law requires it, are you willing to bear arms on behalf of the United States?	Yes. I am willing to serve in the U.S. military and use a weapon.
	If the law requires it, are you willing to perform noncombatant services in the U.S. Armed Forces?	Yes. I am willing to serve in the U.S. military and not use a weapon.
	If the law requires it, are you willing to perform work of national importance under civilian direction?	Yes. I am willing to do work to help my community, my state, or the country during an emergency.

Voices of Freedom

Interview Practice 45: Matching

Match the question and the correct answer.

_____ 1. Do you understand the full Oath of Allegiance to the United States?

a. Yes. I am willing to serve in the U.S. military and use a weapon.

_____ 2. If the law requires it, are you willing to bear arms on behalf of the United States?

b. Yes. I am ready to promise to be loyal only to the United States, to support the Constitution and U.S. laws, and to fight or work for the United States if needed.

_____ 3. Do you support the Constitution and form of government of the United States?

c. Yes. I understand that I promise to be loyal only to the United States, to support the Constitution and U.S. laws, and to fight or work for the United States if needed.

_____ 4. Are you willing to take the full Oath of Allegiance to the United States?

d. Yes. I am willing to serve in the U.S. military and not use a weapon.

_____ 5. If the law requires it, are you willing to perform work of national importance under civilian direction?

e. Yes. I believe in the Constitution as the supreme law of the land, and I believe in our form of government.

_____ 6. If the law requires it, are you willing to perform noncombatant services in the U.S. Armed Forces?

f. Yes. I am willing to do work to help my community, my state, or the country during an emergency.

VOICES of FREEDOM
Interview Practice 46: Matching

Match the picture and the correct question. Then answer the question with your own information.

_____ 1.

a. If the law requires it, are you willing to perform noncombatant services in the U.S. Armed Forces?

_____ 2.

b. Do you support the Constitution and form of government of the United States?

_____ 3.

c. If the law requires it, are you willing to perform work of national importance under civilian direction?

_____ 4.

d. Are you willing to take the full Oath of Allegiance to the United States?

_____ 5.

e. If the law requires it, are you willing to bear arms on behalf of the United States?

Voices of Freedom
Practice Test 1

Student's Name _____ I.D. Number _____

Course _____ Teacher _____ Date _____

A. CIVICS QUESTIONS

1. What does the Constitution do?

   _____

2. What do we call the first ten amendments to the Constitution?

   _____

3. Name one branch or part of the government.

   _____

4. What are two rights in the Declaration of Independence?

   _____

5. How many U.S. Senators are there?

   _____

6. We elect a U.S. Representative for how many years?

   _____

7. Under our Constitution, some powers belong to the federal government.
   What is one power of the federal government?

   _____

8. How many justices are on the Supreme Court?

   _____

9. What is one responsibility that is only for United States citizens?

   _____

10. Who lived in America before the Europeans arrived?

    _____

11. What happened at the Constitutional Convention?

    _____

12. Name one war fought by the United States in the 1800s.

    _____

13. Who was President during World War I?

    _____

14. What did Martin Luther King, Jr. do?

_____

15. Name one state that borders Mexico.

_____

16. Why does the flag have thirteen stripes?

_____

B. INTERVIEW QUESTIONS

Answer the questions.

1. On what date did you become a permanent resident?

_____

2. Are either of your parents U.S. citizens?

_____

3. When was the last time you left the United States? How long were you absent?
Where did you go? Why?

_____

C. READING

Say the questions.

1. Who was the first President of the United States?
2. What are the colors on the American flag?
3. When is Memorial Day?

D. WRITING

Listen and write the sentence you hear.

1. _____
2. _____
3. _____

Score: _____ correct x **4 points** = _____

VOICES of FREEDOM
Practice Test 2

Student's Name _____	I.D. Number _____
Course _____ Teacher _____	Date _____

A. CIVICS QUESTIONS

1. What is the supreme law of the land?

   _____

2. What is an amendment?

   _____

3. What are the two parts of the U.S. Congress?

   _____

4. What is freedom of religion?

   _____

5. The House of Representatives has how many voting members?

   _____

6. We elect a U.S. Senator for how many years?

   _____

7. Under our Constitution, some powers belong to the states. What is one power of the states?

   _____

8. What is the highest court in the United States?

   _____

9. Name one right only for United States citizens.

   _____

10. Why did the colonists fight the British?

   _____

11. Who wrote the Declaration of Independence?

   _____

12. Name the U.S. war between the North and the South.

   _____

13. Before he was President, Eisenhower was a general. What war was he in?

   _____

14. What movement tried to end racial discrimination?

   _____

15. Where is the Statue of Liberty?

   _____

16. What is the name of the national anthem?

   _____

B. INTERVIEW QUESTIONS

Answer the questions.

   1. How long have you been a permanent resident?

   _____

   2. Are you currently employed? What's your position?

   _____

   3. When was your most recent trip outside the United States? How long were you gone? Where did you travel? What was the reason for the trip?

   _____

C. READING

Say the questions.

   1. Who lives in the White House?
   2. When do people in the United States vote for President?
   3. What city in the United States has the most people?

D. WRITING

Listen and write the sentence you hear.

   1. _____
   2. _____
   3. _____

Score: _____ correct x **4 points** = _____

ANSWER KEY

READING, WRITING, & CIVICS PRACTICE

UNIT A
Page 2   Reading Practice
B. 1. is
2. first
3. be
4. for
5. United States
6. state
7. is
8. first
9. of
10. citizen

UNIT B
Page 4   Reading Practice
B. 1. name
2. city
3. state
4. country
5. citizens
6. first
7. are
8. is
9. country
10. citizens

UNIT 1
Page 6   Reading Practice
B. 1. south
2. capital
3. largest
4. has
5. the
6. people
7. of
8. is
9. state
10. north

Page 7   Civics Practice
A. 1. e   5. g
2. h   6. c
3. a   7. b
4. f   8. d

B. 1. b   3. a
2. d   4. c

UNIT 2
Page 9   Reading Practice
B. 1. flag
2. states
3. largest
4. capital
5. people
6. is
7. American
8. have
9. state
10. United States

Page 10   Civics Practice
A. 1. b   3. d
2. c   4. a

B. 1. flag
2. United States
3. to
4. for
5. one
6. and

UNIT 3
Page 12   Reading Practice
B. 1. United States
2. Senators
3. President
4. White House
5. capital
6. lives
7. meet
8. Washington, D.C.
9. the
10. of

Page 13   Civics Practice
A. 1. c
2. a
3. b

B. 1. legislative
2. judicial
3. executive
4. checks
5. President

C. 1. b
2. c
3. a

UNIT 4
Page 15   Reading Practice
B. 1. United States
2. vote
3. Senators
4. citizens
5. elects
6. vote
7. people
8. Congress
9. elects
10. the

Page 16   Civics Practice
A. 1. e   4. f
2. a   5. c
3. d   6. b

B. 1. d   4. e
2. f   5. a
3. b   6. c

C. 1. 435
2. 2
3. 4
4. 100
5. 6

UNIT 5
Page 18   Reading Practice
B. 1. people
2. President
3. elects
4. one
5. votes
6. votes
7. Congress
8. citizens
9. White House
10. in, of

Page 19   Civics Practice
1. e   7. j
2. i   8. d
3. a   9. b
4. l   10. k
5. g   11. f
6. c   12. h

UNIT 6
Page 21   Reading Practice
B.
1. Thanksgiving
2. people
3. first
4. is
5. come
6. was
7. come
8. lived
9. Columbus Day
10. want

Page 22   Civics Practice
A.
1. d   4. b
2. c   5. a
3. e

B.
1. c
2. a
3. b

C.
1. b
2. c
3. a

D.
1. d
2. a
3. b
4. c

UNIT 7
Page 24   Reading Practice
B.
1. is
2. President
3. right
4. George Washington
5. United States
6. President
7. was
8. Independence Day
9. have
10. capital

Page 25   Civics Practice
A.
1. b   4. c
2. f   5. e
3. d   6. a

B.
1. d   4. e
2. c   5. a
3. b

UNIT 8
Page 27   Reading Practice
B.
1. was
2. United States
3. first
4. Father of Our Country
5. state
6. President
7. city
8. George Washington
9. dollar bill
10. capital

Page 28   Civics Practice
1. d   7. k
2. g   8. e
3. b   9. a
4. l   10. h
5. i   11. f
6. c   12. j

UNIT 9
Page 30   Reading Practice
B.
1, is
2. right
3. President
4. state
5. vote
6. largest
7. have
8. Presidents' Day
9. citizen
10. Abraham Lincoln

Page 31   Civics Practice
1. h   8. m
2. n   9. c
3. b   10. g
4. l   11. e
5. f   12. i
6. k   13. d
7. a   14. j

UNIT 10
Page 33   Reading Practice
B.
1. is   7. vote
2. come   8. Name
3. citizens   9. Labor Day
4. right   10. United
5. vote   States
6. people

Page 34   Civics Practice
A.
1. f   4. a
2. d   5. e
3. b   6. c

B.
1. c   4. b
2. a   5. d
3. e

UNIT 11
Page 36   Reading Practice
B.
1. is
2. Memorial
3. Labor Day
4. President
5. lives
6. is
7. Independence
8. Presidents' Day
9. of
10. Washington

Page 37   Civics Practice
1. d   8. b
2. i   9. l
3. m   10. f
4. k   11. e
5. a   12. h
6. j   13. g
7. c

UNIT 12
Page 39   Reading Practice
B.
1. vote
2. citizens
3. President
4. right
5. pay
6. elect
7. can
8. taxes
9. vote
10. have

Page 40   Civics Practice
A.
1. d   4. f
2. e   5. c
3. a   6. b

B.
1. c   4. e
2. a   5. b
3. d

INTERVIEW PRACTICE

Page 43
Interview Practice 2

1. b   4. a
2. d   5. f
3. e   6. c

Page 47
Interview Practice 4

1. e   4. f
2. d   5. c
3. a   6. b

Page 51
Interview Practice 6

1. e   4. b
2. c   5. d
3. a

Page 55
Interview Practice 8

1. c   4. f
2. e   5. d
3. a   6. b

Page 59
Interview Practice 10

1. b   4. a
2. d   5. c
3. f   6. e

Page 63
Interview Practice 12

1. c   4. e
2. f   5. a
3. b   6. d

Page 67
Interview Practice 14

1. d   4. c
2. a   5. b
3. e

Page 71
Interview Practice 16

1. d   4. b
2. a   5. f
3. e   6. c

Page 75
Interview Practice 18

1. e   4. b
2. c   5. d
3. a

Page 79
Interview Practice 20

1. c
2. a
3. d
4. b

Page 80
Interview Practice 21

1. g   5. d
2. b   6. a
3. c   7. f
4. e

Page 81
Interview Practice 22

1. g   5. c
2. e   6. d
3. h   7. a
4. b   8. f

Page 85
Interview Practice 24

1. e   4. b
2. a   5. d
3. f   6. c

Page 86
Interview Practice 25

1. d   4. a
2. e   5. c
3. b   6. f

Page 89
Interview Practice 27

1. e   4. f
2. d   5. b
3. a   6. c

Page 90
Interview Practice 28

1. f   4. c
2. d   5. e
3. a   6. b

Page 93
Interview Practice 30

1. d   4. e
2. f   5. c
3. a   6. b

Page 94
Interview Practice 31

1. c   4. e
2. f   5. b
3. a   6. d

Page 97
Interview Practice 33

1. e   4. f
2. d   5. c
3. a   6. b

Page 98
Interview Practice 34

1. b   4. c
2. e   5. f
3. a   6. d

Page 101
Interview Practice 36

1. c   4. f
2. e   5. b
3. a   6. d

Page 102
Interview Practice 37

1. d   4. f
2. c   5. b
3. a   6. e

Page 105
Interview Practice 39

1. c   4. b
2. e   5. d
3. a

Page 106
Interview Practice 40

1. c   4. b
2. e   5. d
3. a

Page 109
Interview Practice 42

1. d   4. e
2. c   5. b
3. a

Page 110
Interview Practice 43

1. b   4. a
2. e   5. c
3. d

Page 113
Interview Practice 45

1. c   4. b
2. a   5. f
3. e   6. d

Page 114
Interview Practice 46

1. e   4. b
2. d   5. c
3. a

PRACTICE TESTS A & B
(Pages 115–118)

A. Civics Questions
Have students find the correct answers on *Voices of Freedom* Student Book pages 228–237 ("100 Civics Test Questions").

B. Interview Questions
Answers will vary.

C. Reading
Students read the sentences aloud.

D. Writing
Read each sentence twice and have students write what they hear.

Practice Test A:
1. Columbus Day is in October.
2. The flag is red, white, and blue.
3. Canada is north of the United States.

Practice Test B:
1. Thanksgiving is in November.
2. President Washington is on the dollar bill.
3. Mexico is south of the United States.